KIDS' TRAVEL GUIDE

SKI

SPECIAL EDITION!

KIDS' TRAVEL GUIDE
SKI

Author: Lisa Marie Mercer
Editor: Carma Graber
Graphic designer: Francesca Guido
Published by FlyingKids

Visit us @ **www.theflyingkids.com**

Contact us: **leonardo@theflyingkids.com**

ISBN: 978-1-910994-70-2

Acknowledgments
Key: t=top; b=bottom; l=left, r=right; c=center; m=main image; bg=background
All images are from **Shutterstock or public domain except those mentioned below.**
Designed by freepik.com: 35bg, 37bg, 38bg, 39bg, 40bg
Attributions: 15mcr-By Jon Wick (originally posted to Flickr as Go Time) [CC BY 2.0 (http://creativecommons.org/licenses/by/2.0)], via Wikimedia Commons; 15mr-By EncMstr (EncMstr) [GFDL (http://www.gnu.org/copyleft/fdl.html), CC BY-SA-3.0 (http://creativecommons.org/licenses/by-sa/3.0/) or CC BY-SA 2.5-2.0-1.0 (http://creativecommons.org/licenses/by-sa/2.5-2.0-1.0)], via Wikimedia Commons; 15mbl-By Rama (Own work) [CC BY-SA 2.0 fr (http://creativecommons.org/licenses/by-sa/2.0/fr/deed.en)], via Wikimedia Commons; 25m-2nd-By EncMstr (EncMstr photography, and annotated with Photoshop) [GFDL (http://www.gnu.org/copyleft/fdl.html), CC BY-SA-3.0 (http://creativecommons.org/licenses/by-sa/3.0/) or CC BY-SA 2.5-2.0-1.0 (http://creativecommons.org/licenses/by-sa/2.5-2.0-1.0)], via Wikimedia Commons; 34ml-By Keanu @ no:wp (Own work) [GFDL (http://www.gnu.org/copyleft/fdl.html) or CC BY-SA 3.0 (http://creativecommons.org/licenses/by-sa/3.0)], via Wikimedia Commons.

TABLE OF CONTENTS

Dear Parents,

If you bought this book, you're probably planning a family ski trip with your kids. You are spending a lot of time and money in the hopes that this family vacation will be pleasant and fun. You would like your children to learn a little about skiing or snowboarding, including the techniques and some of the history. You hope they will always remember the trip as a very special experience.

The reality is often quite different. Parents may find themselves frustrated as they struggle to convince their kids to snap into their bindings and play in the snow. Meanwhile, the kids just want to watch TV. Or the children are glued to their mobile devices instead of enjoying the new sights and scenery. Many parents are disappointed after they return home and discover that their kids don't remember much about the trip and the new things they learned.

A family ski vacation is fun. But difficulties can arise when children are not in their natural environment and need to learn new and unfamiliar skills. *Kids' Travel Guide – Ski* takes this into account and supports children as they get ready for the trip, visit the ski resort, learn to ski and snowboard, and finally, return home.

Kids' Travel Guide – Ski offers general information about the sports of skiing and snowboarding, the terminology, the trail ratings, the gear, and how to stay safe. It also includes puzzles, tasks to complete, useful tips, and other recommendations along the way. All of this encourages children to experiment, explore, and be more involved in the family's ski vacation—as well as to learn new information about skiing and make memories throughout the vacation.

In addition, kids are asked to document and write about their experiences during the vacation, so that when you return home, they will have a memoir that will be fun to look at and reread again and again.

HAVE A GREAT AND SAFE SKI VACATION!

Hi, Kids!

If you are reading this book, it means you are lucky—you are going on a ski vacation! You probably already know where you are going, and you may have noticed that your parents are getting ready for the journey.

But what about you? Don't worry, this is not just another guidebook for your parents. This book is for you only—for the future skiing or snowboarding champion!

So what is this book all about?

First and foremost, meet Leonardo, your very own personal ski guide on this vacation. Leonardo has visited many places around the world, and he knows a lot about skiing and snowboarding. He'll tell you everything you need to know to have a great ski trip! You'll find his tips and ideas, fun quizzes, and other surprises throughout the book.

Leonardo will also help you pack and get ready to leave. He'll stay in the ski resort with you (don't worry, it doesn't cost more money)! And he will see the sights and have fun with you until you return home. So let's prepare to hit the slopes ☺ !

HAVE FUN!

THE BEGINNING

Going skiing and snowboarding

We are going to ski in _____ (country).

Name of the city where we'll stay: _____

How will you get there? By plane / car / train / other_____

Where will you stay? _____

Is this your first visit? _____

Are you going to ski or snowboard? _____

What else do you expect to do?_____

_____

Are you excited about the trip?

This is an excitement indicator. Ask each of your family members how excited they are (from *"not at all"* up to *"very, very much"*), and mark it down on the indicator. Leonardo marked the level of his excitement …

not at all   Leonardo ^{very very much!}

Who is going on our ski trip?

Write down the names of family members traveling with you.

Name:

Age:

Ski or snowboard level (beginner/intermediate/expert):

What is the most exciting thing about your upcoming trip?

Name:

Age:

Ski or snowboard level (beginner/intermediate/expert):

What is the most exciting thing about your upcoming trip?

Name:

Age:

Ski or snowboard level (beginner/intermediate/expert):

What is the most exciting thing about your upcoming trip?

Name:

Age:

Ski or snowboard level (beginner/intermediate/expert):

What is the most exciting thing about your upcoming trip?

Paste a picture of your family.

Mom and Dad will probably do a lot of the packing. So Leonardo will only tell you the special stuff you might want to take on your ski vacation.

He has made a list, so you can check things off as you pack them:

❄ *Kids' Travel Guide—Ski*—of course!

❄ Your ski equipment, if you have it. (If you don't, no worries—Mom or Dad will rent it for you.)

❄ Snow boots

❄ Comfortable walking shoes

❄ Extra socks and gloves

❄ A scarf for your neck

❄ A hat, sunglasses, and ski goggles

❄ Pens and pencils

❄ Crayons and markers (It is always nice to color and paint.)

❄ A book to read

❄ Your smart phone/camera/tablet

❄ A notebook or writing pad (You can use it for games or writing, or to draw or doodle in when you're bored ...)

Leonardo's fitness plan

Getting ready for a ski vacation is not just about packing warm clothes. You have to train and get in shape! Leonardo has some fun exercises to prepare you for the slopes.

Skiing and snowboarding are all about balance. You can practice your balance with these activities:

○ Play hopscotch
○ Jump rope
○ Roller-skate
○ Ride your skateboard
○ Ice-skate
○ Ride a bicycle
○ Take dance lessons

Put a check mark by the ones you tried. Were they easy? Maybe you already have great balance! But Leonardo has some fun games to make your balance even better.

Beanbag walk:

● Place a beanbag on your shoulder and walk around the room.

● Next, walk with the beanbag on top of your head.

● Here comes the challenge! Balance the beanbag at the top of one foot—on your ankle—and try to walk. You will need to lift your toes off the ground to keep the bag in place. This game will make your ankles stronger for skiing and snowboarding.

One-legged catch:

● Have your family members stand in a circle.

● Toss the beanbag to each other. Anyone who drops the bag has to stand on one leg until they catch it again.

● If they drop the beanbag a second time, they have to stand on one leg with one hand behind their head until they catch it.

Leonardo has appointed you to be your family's personal trainer! Before the trip, get your family together and teach them these exercises.

To **Ski** or to **Snowboard?**
That is the question ...!

And that's a very good question ☺! Because both are so much fun! Some people can't decide until they try them both. Leonardo loves both sports, but he has some ideas to help you choose.

Which sounds more fun to you?

- ○ Surfing, wakeboarding, and skateboarding! **Then you'll like snowboarding**.
- ○ Roller-skating, water-skiing, and ice-skating! **Then you'll like skiing**.

Which sounds cooler?

- ○ Both my feet will be on one board. Snowboarding
- ○ My feet will be on two different boards. Skiing
- ○ Using Poles. Skiing
- ○ A very old sport? Skiing
- ○ A sort of new sport? Snowboarding

Most people think snowboarding began in the 1970s. Turn the page to find out the real history of the sport ...

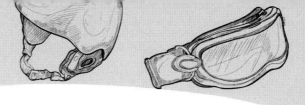

The history of **snowboarding—** and a **teenager's invention**

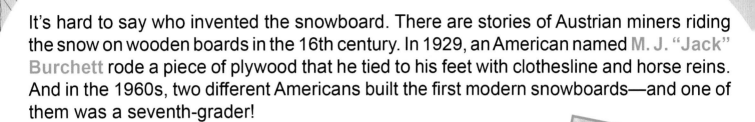

It's hard to say who invented the snowboard. There are stories of Austrian miners riding the snow on wooden boards in the 16th century. In 1929, an American named M. J. "Jack" Burchett rode a piece of plywood that he tied to his feet with clothesline and horse reins. And in the 1960s, two different Americans built the first modern snowboards—and one of them was a seventh-grader!

In 1963, Tom Sims created a ski-board in his seventh-grade shop class. The board combined his two favorite activities: skiing and skateboarding!

Then on Christmas morning 1965, a man named Sherman Poppen connected two water skis, added a leash, and created the "Snurfer." Poppen and his family were surfers. The Snurfer let them surf on the snow!

Did you know?

Tom Sims was a stunt double* in the James Bond movie *A View to a Kill*, which helped make the snowboard popular.

*A stunt double is someone who looks somewhat like a certain movie actor. If that actor can't perform a skill (like snowboarding) the stunt double does it instead—and the audience doesn't know the difference!

Tom Sims is credited with many of the most important innovations in both snowboarding and skateboarding—including the first metal-edged snowboard and the first snowboarding half-pipe.

Q: WHAT OFTEN FALLS IN THE WINTER BUT NEVER GETS HURT?

A: SNOW.

Skiing's long history—
From **wartime** to **fun times!**

Did you know that skiing is thousands of years old? Historians found the first known pair of skis in Russia. It's thought that the skis date back to 6300 BC!

The historians also discovered ancient pieces of skis in Scandinavian countries like Norway, Sweden, and Finland.

Back then, the Scandinavians used skiing for transportation and for warfare.

Did you know?

The word for ski comes from the Norwegian word *skio*, which means "wooden stick."

Skiing in Scandinavian mythology

The people of the Scandinavian countries worshipped Ullr, the God of Snow, and Skadi, the Goddess of Winter. According to legend, Ullr was an amazing skier. He would streak across the sky and leave a stream of glittering stars in his tracks!

In January, some ski resorts celebrate Ullr Fest. People dress up in silly Viking costumes and parade through the streets.

Skadi, the winter goddess, was a very powerful woman—but the other gods tricked her into marrying Njord, the God of the Sea. Njord liked to live by the sea. But Skadi was only happy in the mountains. Their marriage didn't last very long.

Some legends say that Skadi eventually married Ullr. Do you think they would have lived happily ever after 😊?

How skiing **became popular ...**

In its early history, skiing was a big part of wars, and ski soldiers were important fighters. Then in 1800, things started to change. In a Norwegian town called Telemark, people decided that skiing was also a fun thing to do. They turned it into a popular sport.

Did you know?

"Telemark" is a kind of skiing that was invented in the town of Telemark, Norway. In telemark skiing, only the toe of the ski boot attaches to the binding.

Skiing comes to the United States

During the 1800s, many Norwegian skiers moved to the United States, and they taught people to ski. Snowshoe Thompson, (born Jon Thorsteinson Rui) moved to the United States when he was 10 years old. He became a mail carrier during the California Gold Rush. Can you guess how he delivered the mail from town to town? If you said on skis, you are correct ☺ !

Did you know?

Skiing became an Olympic sport in 1928. That's when the first official Winter Olympics were held in France.

Skiing during World War II

Ski soldiers were also important during World War II. Many of the battles were fought in the mountains of Italy. The US Army trained a group of men called the 10th Mountain Division to engage in mountain warfare. Just like the warriors of long ago, these men used their skis to travel through the mountains. When they came home, many of them opened ski resorts in the United States.

DRAW A TRAIL OF STARS BEHIND ULLR.

COLOR SKADI'S OUTFIT.

Do you speak "ski" or "snowboard"?

Skiing and snowboarding have their own language! Leonardo wants to teach you some of the most common terms.

Alpine skiing: Downhill skiing (as opposed to cross-country skiing).

Brain bucket: Slang for ski helmet. It's called a brain bucket because it protects your head from injury.

Carving: Tipping your ski or snowboard onto its edge.

Catch air: An advanced jump performed by professional skiers and snowboarders.

Goofy: A snowboarder who rides with his or her right foot in front.

Regular: A snowboarder who rides with his or her left foot in front (the opposite of goofy).

Terrain park: An area of the resort that contains features such as boxes, rails, slides, and jumps.

Yard sale: A fall that causes your boards to come off and scatters your poles and other belongings around the slope.

Quizzes!

Write the correct term under each picture.

1

2

3

4

5

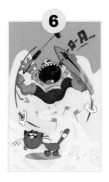

6

7

8

ANSWERS:
1-Brain bucket
2-Carving
3-Alpine skiing
4-Terrain park
5-Goofy
6-Yard sale
7-Regular
8-Catch air

15

Know your **SNOW**

Is there snow in the place you live? Yes / No

Do you like snow?

Before you learned to ski or snowboard, you might have thought that snow was snow, and that it's all pretty much the same.

Once you take your ski trip, you will become an expert on the many different types of snow.

Here are some examples:

- **Artificial snow** – When Mother Nature refuses to provide snow, ski resorts bring out the snow cannons and fill the slopes with artificial snow.

- **Brown snow** – During spring, the mud shows through the melting snow, making it look really yucky.

- **Chowder** – This heavy, wet, lumpy snow looks like clam chowder.

- **Moguls** – A series of bumps in the snow. Advanced skiers and snowboarders love mogul skiing.

- **Corduroy** – When the Snowcats (trucks made to travel over snow) groom the ski trails, they create patterns that look like corduroy pants.

- **Powder** – That deep fluffy stuff that comes from a big snowstorm.

Did you know?
Eskimos have more than 40 different words for snow!

Quizzes! Name the type of snow in each picture:

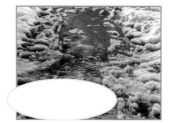

Green, blue, red, black:
Leonardo Explains the trail signs

Have you ever wondered which trails you should ski on? Every ski trail has a color code, which tells you if it is for beginners, intermediates, or experts.

Your riding buddy tells you that he can "do the blacks."

What is he talking about? Ski resorts have a rating system that tells you how hard each trail is.

- **Green** is the easiest. All beginners learn on green trails.
- **Blue** trails are more difficult. Once you master the basic skills, you will be able to ski or ride on these intermediate trails.
- **Black** trails are for expert skiers and snowboarders.

So what about **red**? If you're asking about red, you're probably skiing in Europe. On European slopes, red trails are harder than blue trails but easier than black trails.

Quizzes!

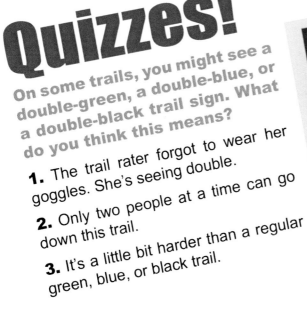

On some trails, you might see a double-green, a double-blue, or a double-black trail sign. What do you think this means?

1. The trail rater forgot to wear her goggles. She's seeing double.

2. Only two people at a time can go down this trail.

3. It's a little bit harder than a regular green, blue, or black trail.

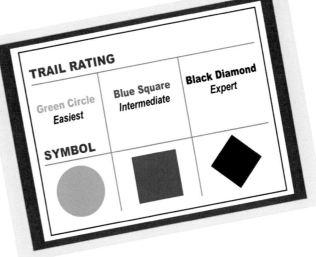

TRAIL RATING		
Green Circle Easiest	Blue Square Intermediate	Black Diamond Expert
SYMBOL		

ANSWER:

3. It's a little bit harder than a regular green, blue, or black trail.

Did you know?

A trail's rating depends on the resort. A black trail at a small ski area might be rated blue at a larger resort.

Keep skiing fun ...
Follow the responsibility code

Leonardo wants you to stay safe. That's why he wants you to memorize the responsibility code.

1. Always stay in control—be able to stop and to avoid other people or objects.

2. People ahead of you have the right of way. It's your responsibility to avoid them.

3. Never stop where you will be blocking the trail, or where you can't be seen from above.

4. Whenever you start downhill or merge into a trail, look uphill and yield to others.

5. Always use devices to help prevent runaway equipment.

6. Obey all signs and warnings. Keep off closed trails and out of closed areas.

7. Before you use any lift, you must know how to load, ride, and unload safely.

TIP! Be careful—the Ski Patrol can take away your lift ticket if you disobey any of these safety rules.

Q: WHAT DO YOU CALL BATMAN AND ROBIN AFTER THEY GET RUN OVER BY A SNOWCAT?

A: FLATMAN AND RIBBON.

Safety

1. Leonardo is skiing down the slope. How fast should he go?
    a. As fast as he can.
    b. Only as fast as he can go and still have control.

2. A little girl is standing in the middle of the trail. What should Leonardo do?
    a. Make a turn to avoid her.
    b. Knock her over.

3. A trail is roped off. Should Leonardo duck under it?
    a. Sure! It will be fun to have the trail to himself!
    b. No! It's probably dangerous!

4. What will happen if Leonardo ducks under the ropes?
    a. He'll win a medal.
    b. The Ski Patrol will take away his lift ticket.

5. Leonardo sees his friends on the slope. Should he stop and talk with them?
    a. Yes, it's important to be friendly.
    b. Yes, but they should all move to the side of the slope.

6. What is the color of the most difficult trail? Color it.

7. What is the color of the easiest trail? Color it.

8. What is the color of your trail? Color it.

Answers: 1. B; 2. A; 3. B; 4. B; 5. B; 6. Black; 7. Green

Putting on your Ski Boots

Some people say that putting on your boots is the hardest part of skiing. Leonardo will help you practice … 😮

To put on your ski boots, follow these steps:

- ✅ Put on your special ski socks. Make sure that they aren't bunched up.
- ✅ Unbuckle the boots. Mom and Dad might need to help you the first time.
- ✅ Pull the tongue of the boot forward.
- ✅ Slide your foot into the boot.
- ✅ Stomp your heel, as if you are having temper tantrum. This is one time that it's okay to do that!
- ✅ Fasten the strap at the top of your boot.
- ✅ Buckle your boots, starting with the ankle buckle, and then work your way to the top.

How easy or hard was it to put on your boots the first time?

VERY EASY   VERY HARD

How easy or hard was it for you the last time?

VERY EASY   VERY HARD

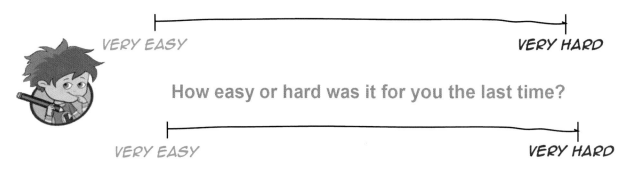

Walking in ski boots is even harder than putting them on. But Leonardo has some ideas for making it easier:

1. Unbuckle the top buckle.
2. Find the lever in the back of your boot. Switch it from "ski" to "walk."
3. Walk slowly, placing your heel down first and then your toes.
4. When walking downstairs, turn sideways and hold on to the railing.

TIP!

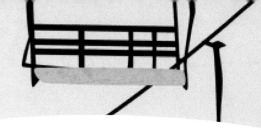

All about the all-important **lift ticket**

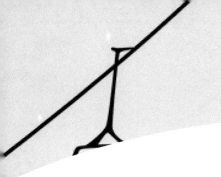

Take a look at your lift ticket. It has a special barcode. The lift operators use a cool device to scan it. This tells them that your mom or dad has paid for your ticket.

When you watch the people in front of you, you will notice that it sometimes takes a very long time for the attendant to scan their tickets. That's because some people choose to attach their tickets to their middle layers of clothing.

It's best to attach your lift ticket to one of the side zippers on your ski jacket. Some jackets even come with special lift ticket clips.

Attaching your ticket

The person at the ticket window will give you a ticket and a zip-tie.

1. Find the hole punched at the top of your ticket.

2. Thread the zip-tie through the hole.

3. Thread the zip-tie through the attachment on your side-pocket zipper.

4. Make sure that the barcode is facing out.

Did you know?
Cool people call lift attendants "lifties."

TIP!
Never attach your lift ticket to the main zipper on your jacket. When the wind blows, it will flap around and hit you in the face!

Look at your ski jacket. Find the best place to attach your lift ticket.

I will attach my lift ticket to my

_____.

Pizza and french fries:
not just for lunch

On your first day at the ski slopes, you might hear the instructors yelling *"Pizza"* or *"French fries!"* No, it's not lunchtime. The instructor is talking about **two positions in skiing**.

Pizza

In the pizza position, your ski tips face each other, and the tails of your skis point outward. Its real name is the "wedge."
This is the position you learn when you first start skiing. Since you go much slower in the wedge position, it's easier to learn the basics.

French fries

Do you know what parallel lines are? Two lines that are the same distance apart and never meet (like railroad tracks).
In skiing, french fries means the parallel position. Once you learn how to make turns in the wedge position, you will advance to parallel skiing.

The cool class: ski and snowboard school

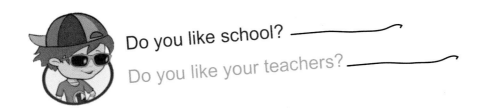

Do you like school?

Do you like your teachers?

Now … Do you like to have fun? Do you like to play in the snow?
How would you like to fly in the mountains? What about dancing in the snow? 😊
Do you know where you can learn to do all that?
At ski or snowboard school!

Did you know?

Ski school is not just for learning to ski. You will make new friends from all over the world! Even better, the instructors know all the cool, secret places on the mountain!

Making the most of your lesson:
A few tips that will help you enjoy it more!

- Stay with your group at all times.
- Remember your instructor's name. If you get lost, go up to another ski class and tell them your instructor's name.
- Never try to hold on to your instructor when you get off the lifts. You will both fall down.
- Your instructor may have each of you ski or snowboard down the hill one by one.
- Keep Mom and Dad's cell phone number in your pocket. Give a copy to your instructor.

 After your lesson, take Mom and Dad to your favorite secret trails! 😊

Check your ski stance

What is a "ski stance"?

Your ski instructor will probably talk to you about your ski stance and alignment. This means "the way you stand on your skis, and how the bones of your body stack on top of each other."

The way you stand on your skis is much different from the way you stand normally. In skiing, your shin bone—the bone in your lower leg—should stay close to the tongue of your ski boot.

How do you know if you're in the right position?

Leonardo suggests the Jumping Test 😊

- Put on your skis and stand in the french fry position.
- Bend your knees, and press your shins against the tongue of your ski boot.
- Jump!

What happened? Were you able to get off the ground?
If yes, you were in the right position 😊.
If no, you are probably skiing with your calves too close to the back of your boots 😳.

Want to know why ski stance is important?

Your ski tips, or the fronts of your skis, control the direction of your movements on the mountain. The tails, or the backs of your skis, are supposed to follow your tips. When you put more of your weight on your ski tails, you turn these followers into leaders. They are not very good at this, and so your turns look very sloppy.

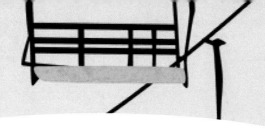
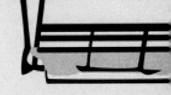

YAY! We get to ride the lifts!

Ski resorts have different types of lifts. Some go all the way to the top of the mountain. Others stay closer to the base area. Leonardo will tell you all about them.

Rope tows: If the resort has a rope tow, hold the rope in one hand and your poles in the other. The rope will pull you up to a small, easy hill.

Magic carpets are like escalators. Just stand up straight and let it pull you up the hill.

Chairlifts: Once your ski skills improve, it's time for the chairlifts. If you are a snowboarder, keep your front foot attached to your board, but leave your back foot loose.

TIP! On the chairlift, both skiers and snowboarders will ride up to a marked line. To get on the chairlift, look over one shoulder and watch the chair approach. As soon as everyone is seated, lower the safety bar. To exit, slide down the short exit ramp, and get out of the way of the next arriving chair.

The gondola: The gondola is an enclosed and sometimes heated cabin. When you load, you place your skis or snowboard in the special slots on the outside of the cabin.

The poma lift: A poma lift is sort of like a rope tow, with one difference. It has a metal plate that you place between your legs. Important: the plate looks like a seat, but it's not. Stay in an upright position for the entire ride. If you sit down, you'll fall backwards!

Ski racing for kids

NASTAR stands for National Standard Race. Almost every ski resort has a NASTAR race course. If you are an intermediate skier, you can compete. You will race against a partner, usually someone close to your own age and skiing level.

The race is not just about going fast. You have to ski around the flags without knocking them over, and without skiing into your opponent's racing trail. This means you have to ski with **control**. And you're not just competing against your opponent. You are competing against all the ski racers your age in the whole country! You might even win a NASTAR medal!

☑ Keep your weight on the front of your boot, like you practiced in the jumping exercise.

☑ Look at the course before you start. Think about where you will turn right, and where you will turn left.

☑ Have fun!

Did you try the NASTAR course? YES / NO ⎯⎯⎯

If yes, how was it? ⎯⎯⎯⎯⎯⎯⎯

⎯⎯⎯⎯⎯⎯⎯⎯⎯⎯⎯

Do you think you could become a ski racer?

☐ YES! I'd like to!

☐ I need to think about it.

☐ No way …

Star in your own ski movie:
Watching Yourself on Video

Your ski instructor or your mom or dad might take videos of you while you ski. These are usually funny to watch, but you can also learn a lot from them. Since you don't have a mirror when you ski or snowboard, it's hard to know if you are doing it correctly. Leonardo always watches himself on video. That's how he became such a great skier!

Take turns watching each other on video.

What did you do right? _____

_____

What do you need to improve? _____

_____

What is an  APRÈS-SKI?

Did you know?
Après means "**after**" in French. So *après-ski* means "**after skiing**."
The accent over the letter "e" means that you pronounce it like "AY". The "s" at the end of a French word is silent.

Here's how to pronounce it: AH-PRAY-Ski.

When does it happen?

Après-ski happens at about 4:30 p.m. Something magic happens on the mountain. Look up, and you'll see a pinkish glow. This is called "alpenglow."

People like to sit outside, drink hot cocoa, and watch the mountain change colors with the sunset. (If you got up early, you could also see alpenglow during the sunrise.) Later, you might toast marshmallows, or sit around the campfire and tell stories.

Quizzes!
By now you have learned many terms and words from the ski world. Try to find them all in this word search puzzle:

- ○ Rope tows
- ○ Pizza
- ○ Ski
- ○ Powder
- ○ Goofy
- ○ Snow
- ○ Leonardo
- ○ Gondolas
- ○ NASTAR

G	I	R	N	S	O	B	A
O	C	O	A	Z	Z	I	P
N	I	K	S	B	C	G	O
D	O	H	T	V	E	O	W
O	S	I	A	O	A	O	D
L	N	S	R	P	A	F	E
A	O	E	I	M	N	Y	R
S	W	O	T	E	P	O	R
O	D	R	A	N	O	E	L

Exploring the village or town

Ask Mom or Dad to take you into the town. Most ski towns have historic buildings and cool museums.

Take a walk through the town with your family.

Can you imagine the town without the snow?

_____

_____

What did you see on your walk?

_____

_____

The town

What does it look like? What special things or places did you find?

_____

_____

The people

What kind of people live there? Are they all local, or are some from other countries? Did you hear different languages?

_____

_____

The shops

What kind of shops did you see? Which one was your favorite?

_____

_____

Was there a ski equipment shop? What kinds of skis and snowboards did you see? Were there any unusual colors, patterns, or shapes?

_____

_____

What do you think about these skis? Give them a new design ☺!

staying at the **ski lodge**

Welcome to the ski lodge!
This is your home during your ski vacation.
You will stay here mostly in the morning
before skiing and the evening after skiing.

Before skiing

Most ski lodges serve a delicious breakfast buffet, with foods such as pancakes, waffles, French toast, rolls, and jams.

What does your lodge look like? ⎯⎯⎯⎯⎯⎯⎯⎯⎯⎯⎯⎯⎯⎯⎯⎯⎯⎯⎯⎯⟶

Does it serve breakfast? ⎯⎯⎯⎯⎯⎯⎯

What did you eat for breakfast? ⎯⎯⎯⎯⎯⎯⎯⎯⎯⎯⎯⎯⎯⎯⎯⎯⎯⎯⎯⟶

When you're done skiing

When you come in after skiing, you can sit by the fireplace and drink hot apple cider. Some ski lodges have a library, where you can borrow books to read during your stay.

Leonardo wants to know what you think of your ski lodge. Pretend you are a travel writer. How many stars would you give to your lodge?

☆ ☆ ☆ ☆ ☆

Explain why you gave it that rating:

⎯⎯⎯⎯⎯⎯⎯⎯⎯⎯⎯⎯⎯⎯⎯⎯⎯⎯⎯⟶

FUN after DARK

At night, the ski resort turns into a winter wonderland! Here are some of the best activities.

Snow and ice sculptures: People from all over the world may compete to see whose sculpture is best!

Fireworks: Some resorts have fireworks on special occasions!

Night skiing: The trails are lit up so that you can ski under the stars!

Torchlight parades: The instructors ski down the mountain holding lit torches.

Put a check mark by the activities your ski resort had.

Were there any special activities not pictured above? List them here:

_____

_____

_____

What to do if ... ?

 Skiing and snowboarding are not easy in the beginning. But Leonardo has some solutions to help you with the problems you might find.

Help ... I can't snap into my bindings.

Don't worry! You probably have snow or ice on the heel of your boot. Slide your foot back and forth over the binding of your ski. Then try to snap in again. If you hear that nice snapping sound, everything is okay. If there's no snap, ask a friend or family member to use their ski pole to scrape off your boot.

Help ... Snow got into my boot and I'm cold.

Leonardo guesses that you have your ski pants bunched up above your ski boots. The inner lining of your ski pants works just like a shower curtain. See the elastic on the bottom? It was made to fit over your boot. This keeps the cold snow from getting into your boot.

Help ... I fell and I'm afraid to get up.

Don't worry! You probably think that you will slide down the hill—out of control—if you get up after a fall. Well, that could only happen if you get up with your skis pointing downhill. After you fall, move your body so that your skis are pointing sideways across the hill.

Help ... Whiteout! The snowboarder in this picture probably can't see very well 👀. This is what happens in a whiteout. Whiteouts occur when it is snowing so much that it's hard to see where you're going. They can be scary, but don't worry—there's a solution! Move toward the edge of the trail. The shadows of the trees will guide you down the hill.

Don't be in a fog …
Your goggles and goggle fog

Quizzes!

You probably noticed that ski outfits include goggles. Can you guess why?

1. They're cool … They look great!

2. They're warm … They will keep my eyes and face from getting cold.

3. They will protect my eyes from the sun's glaring rays.

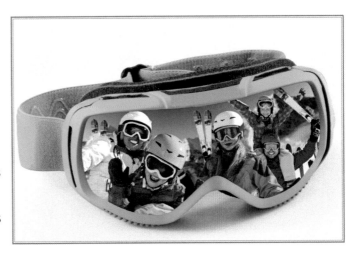

Answer: 3.

If you guessed that your ski goggles protect your eyes from the sun, you're right. But sometimes heat and moisture make the goggles fog up.

Many people pull their goggles up on top of their heads when they get off the slopes. That lets heat and moisture come right in! Why does that happen? Well … hot air rises. If your goggles are on top of your head, all of your body's heat rises up and creates fog.

Don't worry, Leonardo prepared a few tips for preventing goggle fog:

TIP!

- Don't take your goggles off in snow or rain. The moisture will get onto your goggle lenses.
- Put your goggles in your pocket when you go for lunch. You don't want to forget them …
- Don't wipe your goggles with your ski gloves. Instead, go inside to the bathrooms and dry them with the hand dryer or a paper towel.

Q: WHAT DO YOU GET WHEN YOU CROSS A SNOWMAN AND A VAMPIRE?

A: FROSTBITE.

More fun things to do!

There are many things to do in the snow besides skiing and snowboarding. Can you think of some? Leonardo has some ideas …

Quizzes!

Connect a line between the activity and its picture.

A - Sledding

B - Zip-lining

C - Dogsledding

D - Snow biking

E - Snowshoe hiking

F - Snow tubing

Which of these other snow activities would you like to try?

Answers: 1-C; 2-F; 3-E; 4-A; 5-B; 6-D

How much do you know?

1. **Why did Leonardo suggest the beanbag walk?**
   a. To practice your balance.
   b. To practice your cooking skills.
   c. To build strong muscles.

2. **What is a "brain bucket"?**
   a. Slang for new ski shoes in a bucket.
   b. Slang for ski helmet.
   c. That's what you call a smart ski guide.

3. **What is "goofy"?**
   a. A type of ski helmet.
   b. A nickname for a beginner.
   c. A snowboarder who rides with his or her right foot in front.

4. **Who was Tom Sims?**
   a. He created a ski-board.
   b. He was a stunt double in a James Bond movie.
   c. Answers a. and b. are both correct.

5. **The word "ski" comes from …**
   a. The Norwegian word *skio*, which means "wooden stick."
   b. The American word *skidoo*, which means "to depart."
   c. The Swedish word *Skio*, which means "down the hall."

6. **What happened in a Norwegian town called Telemark in 1800?**
   a. The first Winter Olympics were held.
   b. Many Norwegians won medals in the Olympic Games.
   c. People decided that skiing was a fun thing to do, and turned it into a popular sport.

Answers: 1. a; 2. b; 3. c; 4. c; 5. a; 6. c

Even more

SKi TRiVIA

7. What are "chowder," "corduroy," and "powder"?
- a. They are all names of different types of snowboards.
- b. They are all names for different types of snow.
- c. They are all names of ski resorts.

8. Which color of trail is the easiest one for beginners?
- a. Black
- b. Blue
- c. Green

9. What happens if you ignore the safety rules?
- a. The ski patrol can remove your lift ticket.
- b. You will not get hot cocoa at the après-ski.
- c. The ski patrol will take your ski equipment.

10. What do you call the position where your ski tips face each other, and the tails of your skis point outward?
- a. French fries
- b. Pizza
- c. French toast

11. What are "rope tows," "magic carpets," and "gondolas"?
- a. They are all different types of lifts at ski resorts.
- b. They are all different types of ski positions.
- c. They are all different types of ski resorts.

12. What is a french fries position?
- a. It's when you eat french fries during après-ski.
- b. It's when your skis are parallel.
- c. It's when the tails of your skis point outward.

My ski trip JOURNAL

MY CLASS: _____

INSTRUCTOR'S NAME: _____

KIDS IN MY CLASS: _____
_____

BEST FRIEND FROM CLASS: _____
_____

MY FAVORITE TRAILS: _____

My ski trip JOURNAL

DATE	WHAT WE DID ON THE SLOPES	BEST PART

My ski trip

Rating the trip:
Our favorite things

Grade the most beautiful places and the best experiences of your journey:

First Place

Second Place

Third Place

And now, a difficult task—discuss it with your family and decide ...
What did you enjoy most on the trip?